W YOU RATHER

KIDS SERIES

Big Collection of
1200+ Creative Scenarios
& Thought Provoking Questions
for Kids and Family
(6 in 1)

Lucky Sammy

CONTENTS

WOULD YOU RATHER GAME BOOK FOR KIDS 6-12 YEARS OLD: CRAZY JOKES AND CREATIVE SCENARIOS FOR YOUNG INVENTORS.............93

WOULD YOU RATHER GAME BOOK FOR KIDS 6-12 YEARS OLD: CRAZY JOKES AND CREATIVE SCENARIOS FOR ACTIVE KIDS.............122

WOULD YOU RATHER HALLOWEEN GAME BOOK: 200+ CREATIVE QUESTIONS, SPOOKY SCENARIOS & CRAZY CHOICES FOR KIDS 6-12 YEARS OLD.............151

HOW TO PLAY

You will need two to three players, so choose your friends, peers, siblings, cousins or parents and guardians wisely!

The questions should be asked to the whole group and not to each player. It is a fun, intriguing, stimulating, and exciting game where you can find out secrets about your friends & family.

Instincts VS thoughts, thinking VS feeling, emotions VS intellect, beliefs and philosophy VS logic and reason, discovering knowledge VS simple fun; this game has a range of effects!

Try and rely on your instinctual feelings and "gut" responses. What instantly comes to mind? This is the way you should answer. You can use a timer or hourglass, if you and your fellow players need some structure.

Enjoy.

WOULD YOU RATHER

GAME BOOK

For Kids 6-12 Years Old

CRAZY JOKES
AND CREATIVE SCENARIOS
FOR KIDS AND FAMILY

Lucky Sammy

EAT OR DRiNK?

WOULD YOU RATHER...

Eat a chocolate muffin with ketchup
OR
your favourite meal with sugar?

* * *

Eat your least favourite green vegetable every day
OR
a worm once?

* * *

Drink coffee accidentally made with salt
OR
tea accidentally made with jam?

* * *

Eat five burgers in a row
OR
one 24-inch pizza?

* * *

Drink a tomato ice pop
OR
eat the sourest cherry?

* * *

Eat a chocolate bar your dog has slobbered all over
OR
one bite of a snake?

* * *

Eat a protein-packed super green smoothie
OR
a handful of nuts and seeds?

WOULD YOU RATHER...

Drink carrot juice once a week
OR
the strongest health tonic once a year?

* * *

Drink a teaspoon of salty sea water
OR
your worst drink every day for a month?

* * *

Eat a Brussels sprouts sandwich
OR
a peach coated in chocolate?

* * *

Drink coconut coffee every day
OR
eat grass for the rest of your life?

* * *

Eat a mouldy onion
OR
drink only water for 3 weeks?

* * *

Lick a sour lolly
OR
drink a flat & warm fizzy/pop drink?

* * *

Give your last (fave) meal to a homeless person
OR
eat a pickled mackerel?

* * *

Drink one cup of (non-toxic) swamp water
OR
honey water every day for a month?

WOULD YOU RATHER...

Sacrifice all your favourite foods
OR
all of your fave drinks?

* * *

Eat only green vegetables
OR
only your favourite sweets for a week?

* * *

Eat blue cheese (the strongest cheese around!)
OR
the meal you hated when young?

* * *

Eat a jacket potato smothered in Nutella
OR
chips sprinkled with icing sugar?

* * *

Eat the French delicacy "frog's legs"
OR
the South East Asian grilled rat?

* * *

Eat a whole bag of rainbow candy
OR
a giant tub of ice cream?

* * *

Live off pizza for a week
OR
roast dinner for a month?

* * *

Eat a chocolate bar dipped in mayo
OR
a carrot coated with peanut butter?

WOULD YOU RATHER...

Drink flavourless soup for a week
OR
boiled rice every day for a month?

* * *

Drink a litre of cranberry juice
OR
a litre of milk?

* * *

Eat a burger with no sauce
OR
a pizza with no cheese?

* * *

Drink 3 coffees in a row
OR
one large green tea?

* * *

Drink a glass of water with sugar
OR
a cup of vinegar water?

* * *

Eat a handful of beetroot crisps
OR
a whole packet of bbq peanuts?

* * *

Eat only salad for a day
OR
5 Brussels sprouts every day for a week?

ANIMALS

WOULD YOU RATHER...

Be an eagle with a broken wing for a day
OR
a rat for a week?

* * *

Be able to turn your head through 2700 like an owl
OR
see in the dark?

* * *

Explore the seas and oceans freely
OR
soar above the clouds in the sky?

* * *

Live in the rainforest with monkeys
OR
in the Sahara desert?

* * *

Swim like a dolphin with supersonic radar
OR
change colour like a chameleon?

* * *

Be a loyal dog in a loving home
OR
a fiercely independent cat roaming free?

* * *

Be a multi-coloured rainbow frog
OR
an invisible sheep with one eye?

WOULD YOU RATHER...

Transform into a bird
OR
a fish at will?

* * *

Sing like a parrot
OR
howl at the stars like a wolf?

* * *

Have the lifespan of a tortoise
OR
visit your loved ones every day in the future?

* * *

Be a slug with four noses
OR
never be able to jump (like elephants!)?

* * *

Be a capuchin monkey
OR
be a fruit fly?

* * *

Run as fast as a cheetah
OR
swim free in the ocean like a whale?

* * *

Howl like a wolf and be part of a wolf pack
OR
be a sloth?

* * *

Transform into a peacock at will
OR
be a fierce and proud lioness?

WOULD YOU RATHER...

Live as a butterfly for one day
OR
become a beautiful wild tiger for a week?
* * *
Sense vibrations through the ground like an elephant
OR
climb trees like a panther?
* * *
See through the eyes of a dolphin
OR
laugh like a hyena?
* * *
Live as long as a tortoise
OR
live as your favourite animal for one year?
* * *
Be a magical night owl with clear sight
OR
creature of the day and sunlight?
* * *
Be a male lion, the king
OR
a female lion- the huntress?
* * *
Have stripes like a zebra
OR
turn pink like a flamingo?
* * *
Jump like a hare
OR
dig like a badger?

WOULD YOU RATHER...

Live as a hamster for a week
OR
a moth for a month?

* * *

Be a polar bear for a year
OR
a donkey for 3 months?

* * *

Be a wild horse, free to roam
OR
a loved penguin in a zoo?

* * *

Live amongst kangaroos
OR
be a rabbit?

* * *

Become best friends with a dolphin
OR
have 4 dogs?

* * *

See in the dark like a bat
OR
hunt in the night like a panther?

* * *

Hug the earth's largest bear
OR
swim among coral reefs with fish?

SiLLY & WEiRD!

WOULD YOU RATHER...

Become a unicorn for one year
OR
a dragon for one month?
* * *
Be a reindeer as part of Santa's crew
OR
a pixy and live in a forest?
* * *
Tell your crush you love them
OR
give a speech to the entire school?
* * *
Be able to sing like Bob Marley
OR
play the bass guitar like a boss?
* * *
Eat a handful of snow
OR
drink a litre of fizzy pop?
* * *
Be able to grant wishes (like the Genie!)
OR
have the power of invisibility for one day?
* * *
Swim in the ocean like a mermaid
OR
live among the fairies?

WOULD YOU RATHER...

Learn how to play the piano
OR
be able to hold your breath for 5 minutes?

* * *

Visit the moon
OR
travel around the sun in a spaceship?

* * *

Wonder into a desert with a protective shield
OR
climb a mountain?

* * *

Travel around the world in a helicopter
OR
live on a deserted island?

* * *

Count the number of skittle in a jar
OR
watch paint dry for an hour?

* * *

Live in a jungle and eat only fruit
OR
be an Eskimo?

* * *

Go back 5 years into the past
OR
20 years into the future?

* * *

Be a hummingbird for a week
OR
never eat your favourite sweet/treat again?

WOULD YOU RATHER...

Dress like a clown every day for a year
OR
turn up once to school naked?

* * *

Build your own jetpack
OR
swim on the back of a shark?

* * *

Fly in a multi-coloured hot air balloon
OR
jet ski in your funkiest outfit?

* * *

Dance all night to Michael Jackson
OR
attend a gymnastic school for a week?

* * *

Learn how to speak Japanese
OR
live with monks in Thailand?

* * *

Be able to speak to snakes
OR
fly on a broomstick?

* * *

Have your own magical elf
OR
fly on a flying horse?

* * *

Transform into a black dog
OR
a rainbow-coloured cat?

WOULD YOU RATHER...

Be invisible and change invisible at will
OR
walk through walls?

* * *

Speak to trees and listen to their voices
OR
communicate with animals?

* * *

Live in a broom closet for a week
OR
spend a month with your enemy?

* * *

Get stuck in the enchanted flying car
OR
swallow a fly?

* * *

Learn how to stargaze
OR
learn how to predict the future?

* * *

Have your own pet/friend Phoenix
OR
a dragon as a best friend?

* * *

Own a magical sweet shop (with luck potions!)
OR
a dragon's egg?

NATURE

WOULD YOU RATHER...

Walk around the earth and be a world traveller
OR
live in your dream home?
* * *
Live in a magical hobbit-hole in a forest
OR
own a mansion?
* * *
Own an animal shelter caring for dogs & cats
OR
live on top of a mountain?
* * *
Become friends with a bear
OR
ride on the back of a friendly lion?
* * *
Jump off the world's largest waterfall
OR
climb/walk the highest bridge?
* * *
Live in a safari for a week
OR
fly to your favourite country for just one day?
* * *
Visit a butterfly sanctuary
OR
an orangutan wildlife centre?

WOULD YOU RATHER...

Watch a spider spin its web
OR
stare at a jellyfish for an hour?

* * *

Ask a chameleon how s/he changes colour
OR
speak to a parrot?

* * *

Get stuck in a zoo at night
OR
get lost in a nature museum for a day?

* * *

Tell your mum you kissed a snake
OR
hold a tarantula?

* * *

Learn Kung Fu in a Shaolin temple for a year
OR
train with the world's best boxers?

* * *

Become an expert bird watcher
OR
volunteer at a zoo/wildlife sanctuary?

* * *

Climb a tree and watch the sunset
OR
wake up to sunrise on a beach?

* * *

Live in a bamboo hut on a paradise island
OR
own your own boat?

WOULD YOU RATHER...

Own your own island with your favourite musician
OR
inherit a mountain?

* * *

Swim in the world's most beautiful lake
OR
paraglide over inspiring scenery?

* * *

Live off coconuts and mangoes in a foreign country
OR
never be able to leave your own?

* * *

Dive in exquisite coral reefs
OR
have your own private jet?

* * *

Travel the world with your best friends
OR
with your beloved family?

* * *

Own a safari in Africa
OR
a tiger sanctuary in Thailand?

* * *

Come up close to a fruit bat
OR
a huntsman spider?

* * *

Have your own vegetable garden
OR
your own fruit trees?

WOULD YOU RATHER...

Live in a grape orchard
OR
a VIP plane ticket to your fave nature spot?

* * *

Save 40 rabbits
OR
10 dogs from an animal shelter?

* * *

Live in a cave for a week
OR
be lost on a boat at sea for one day?

* * *

Ride a camel through the Egyptian desert
OR
go on an underwater submarine?

* * *

Swim with dolphins
OR
own a pet owl?

* * *

Watch sunset on top of a mountain
OR
live in a hobbit-hole?

* * *

Ride with and bathe elephants
OR
care for monkeys in a conservation centre?

SPACE AND THE UNIVERSE

WOULD YOU RATHER...

Speak to someone who landed on the moon
OR
have your own spaceship?
* * *
Study astronomy (learning about the stars & planets)
OR
live with aliens for a month?
* * *
Only be able to see the beauty of the moon
OR
the light of the sun?
* * *
Live with Albert Einstein for a month
OR
visit Elon Musk's home today?
* * *
Discover your own star and name it
OR
visit a faraway galaxy?
* * *
View the earth from space in an astronaut suit
OR
own the world's best telescope?

WOULD YOU RATHER...

Have your dream home set up in a spaceship
OR
a simple house on earth?
* * *
Live with space scientists for a year
OR
study astrology with astrology experts?
* * *
Travel through a black hole
OR
visit a planet made of light & stardust?
* * *
Live on a planet made of solely oceans
OR
one of solely jungle?
* * *
Travel to the future
OR
travel to the past through time and space?
* * *
Experience a multi-dimensional planet
OR
own planet earth?
* * *
Live on an amazing planet with only animals
OR
travel to the moon with your fave people?
* * *
Find out earth is a secret space station
OR
discover time travel?

WOULD YOU RATHER...

Create your own planet, exactly as you wish
OR
live forever?
* * *
Choose 2 people to explore space with
OR
live in a massive community with strangers?
* * *
Accidentally travel through a space portal
OR
realize how the earth is magic (like in Avatar!)?
* * *
Make objects levitate
OR
wake up every day in space?
* * *
Create a device that allows humans to breathe in space
OR
own your own solar system?
* * *
Work with NASA and become a famous astronaut
OR
find an eternal plant?
* * *
Grow your own food in space
OR
eat only vegetables on earth?
* * *
Get lost in space for an hour
OR
not leave your home for a month?

WOULD YOU RATHER...

Inherit your own planet
OR
go to space camp?

* * *

Own a million dollars on earth
OR
have your own house on the moon?

* * *

Be visited by beings from another planet
OR
live until age 220?

* * *

Go up to space in a rocket
OR
experience a meteorite shower?

* * *

Discover interdimensional space travel
OR
go back in time to change the past?

* * *

Live in a galaxy with 2 suns
OR
3 moons?

* * *

Live in a spaceship as large as planet earth
OR
never be able to return home (to earth)?

* * *

Be able to control water and air
OR
fire and earth?

FAMILY

WOULD YOU RATHER...

Have 1 - 3 brothers and sisters only
OR
12 cousins?!
* * *
Live with all of your family in a simple home
OR
choose only a few in a mansion?
* * *
Win a million dollars and only be allowed one child
OR
have as many children as you wish?
* * *
Give your grandparents a potion that makes them live for
120 years
OR
drink the potion?
* * *
Receive gifts every day
OR
give your family a gift every day?
* * *
Make your own Christmas and birthday cards
OR
be able to buy fancy ones?
* * *
Rewind to a year ago and change something
OR
be a better person now?

WOULD YOU RATHER...

Be seen as kind and generous
OR
talented and gifted?

* * *

Have 5 aunties
OR
5 uncles? (No mixing!)

* * *

Eat Christmas dinner with your family every year
OR
roast potatoes every day?

* * *

Play family monopoly every day
OR
scrabble once a week?

* * *

Go on holiday with your cousins and siblings
OR
parents, aunties and uncles?

* * *

Be a famous solo singer or musician
OR
be part of a successful sibling band?

* * *

Win the lottery and never see your parents again
OR
keep family bonds?

* * *

Sleep in a room with your dad/mum for a month
OR
share a room with your brother/sister for a year?

WOULD YOU RATHER...

Have your mum or dad as a teacher
OR
your older brother or sister?
* * *
Learn a new language with your guardian/parents
OR
inherit a car?
* * *
Discover a hidden basement filled with rats
OR
move house and home constantly?
* * *
Tell your mum and dad your deepest secret
OR
find out your sibling had peed in your bed?
* * *
Sing a song to your entire family
OR
miss out on a special outing?
* * *
Dress in your mum's clothes for a week
OR
not wear underwear for a month?
* * *
Pretend to be a horse in front of grandparents
OR
pretend to speak to walls?
* * *
Laugh like your strangest family member
OR
not laugh for a week?

WOULD YOU RATHER...

Paint your walls any colour
OR
steal all of the hidden sweets?

* * *

Grow up to have your mum's career/profession
OR
your dad's?

* * *

Tell your brother/sister you love them every day
OR
tell them a joke?

* * *

Spend a month on a desert island with your
annoying/weird cousin
OR
never go on holiday?

* * *

Be allowed 5 pets
OR
a friend around for a sleepover every week?

* * *

Give a friend all of your toys
OR
not be allowed to decorate your own room?

* * *

Live in a tent in your garden
OR
eat whatever you like, whenever you like?!

SCHOOL

WOULD YOU RATHER...

Take your least favourite class every day
OR
have your worst teacher for every subject?

* * *

Perform a musical instrument (solo) in front of the whole school
OR
give a speech as part of a group play?

* * *

Sit a Science exam once a week
OR
a Math test every day?

* * *

Take 2 different languages
OR
learn 6 musical instruments?

* * *

Be seen as "teacher's pet"
OR
be part of the popular crowd?

* * *

Boss Art
OR
learn how to cook in Food technology?

* * *

Learn how to be a gymnast
OR
fine-tune your painting skills?

WOULD YOU RATHER...

Write a poem every day
OR
have a sports lesson every day?
* * *
Sit a Religious studies exam every month
OR
read a new literature book every 2 weeks?
* * *
Have 2 - 3 close friends
OR
be part of the cool and "IT" group?
* * *
Share classes with your brother or sister
OR
be seen as talented, gifted, and smart?
* * *
Have your parents know your headmaster/mistress
OR
have a parent as a teacher?
* * *
Have a swimming pool
OR
a fabulous games room at school?
* * *
Have one free period every day
OR
one day off a week? (Forever!)
* * *
Receive average top marks in every class
OR
top marks in your favourite subjects?

WOULD YOU RATHER...

Swap your maths teacher for your science
OR
English teacher?

* * *

Have a muffin or cake every day at lunch
OR
a rainbow-coloured fruit salad?

* * *

Wear a school uniform but have your hair however you
like (including coloured!)
OR
have no uniform?

* * *

Continue your education in your school
OR
go to college elsewhere?

* * *

Be part of your school choir
OR
the netball or football team?

* * *

Tell your teacher you love them
OR
laugh in the middle of assembly?

* * *

Score 100% on a hard test
OR
choose all of your teachers?

* * *

Accidentally have a laughing fit during silence
OR
come to school with blue hair?

WOULD YOU RATHER...

Be allowed to play your fave game during lunch
OR
have an extra hour lunch break?

* * *

Skip 2 years of school
OR
stay and become the best student?

* * *

Take a subject you dislike
OR
miss all breaks for a week?

* * *

Only take science, maths & English
OR
art, music, and drama?

* * *

Be allowed your pet with you at school
OR
never sit exams?

* * *

Marry your school crush
OR
receive a golden ticket to something special?

* * *

Be so good that you get into the top universities
OR
have multiple friends?

WOULD YOU RATHER

GAME BOOK

For Kids 6-12 Years Old

CRAZY JOKES
AND CREATIVE SCENARIOS
FOR YOUNG TRAVELERS

Lucky Sammy

TRANSPORTATION

WOULD YOU RATHER...

Travel to different countries using an airplane
OR
a ship?
* * *
Cross a desert alone with a camel
OR
on foot in a group?
* * *
See the countryside from the sky using a hot air balloon
OR
a paraglider?
* * *
Learn to fly a plane
OR
learn to captain a sailing ship?
* * *
Take a trip on the Trans Siberian Train
OR
the Orient Express?
* * *
Take a tour of a city on a rickshaw
OR
a toboggan?
* * *
Take a gondola ride through Venice
OR
a felucca ride on the Nile river?

WOULD YOU RATHER...

Ride an Indian Elephant
OR
a South African ostrich?

* * *

Zipline over the Grand Canyon
OR
go skydiving?

* * *

Take a tram ride in Los Angeles
OR
a tram ride in Dubai?

* * *

Travel to a remote area in Alaska in a small plane
OR
on a dog sled?

* * *

Tour the countryside on a horse
OR
a bicycle?

* * *

Take a horse carriage to get to your hotel
OR
a tuk-tuk?

* * *

Travel using a magical flying carpet
OR
use a teleporting device?

* * *

Tour Europe with a train
OR
complete Route 66 with a motorcycle?

WOULD YOU RATHER...

Reach the top of a mountain using a cable car
OR
a mule?

* * *

Go canoeing on a lake
OR
white water river rafting?

* * *

Learn to drive a car in a country where they drive on
the opposite side of the road
OR
learn to ride a horse?

* * *

Travel around the world in your own yacht
OR
a private jet?

* * *

Take a ferry ride to the Statue of Liberty
OR
drive over the Seven Mile Bridge?

* * *

Spend a day driving a hovercraft
OR
learning how to use a water jetpack?

* * *

Island hop by using a ferry
OR
a plane?

* * *

Get down a snowy mountain by skiing
OR
using a sled?

WOULD YOU RATHER...

Sit on a bus next to a stranger
OR
ride your bike through an unfamiliar neighborhood?

* * *

Take a bus ride somewhere new with your family
OR
with your friends?

* * *

Get to the other side of a frozen lake by skating over it
OR
walking around it?

* * *

Take a road trip with a car and camp each night
OR
in a motorhome?

* * *

Be able to walk anywhere you want to go without
getting tired
OR
fly and get tired every ten minutes?

* * *

Explore the oceans in a submarine
OR
explore the land from a helicopter?

* * *

Ride a horse through the wild west
OR
a motorcycle through a futuristic city?

COUNTRIES

WOULD YOU RATHER...

Visit a lot of places in one foreign country
OR
visit one place in a lot of countries?

* * *

Only eat local foods in other countries
OR
only food you know from home?

* * *

Travel to other countries but never come back home
OR
never travel to other countries?

* * *

Go to a middle eastern country like Arabia
OR
a far eastern country like China?

* * *

Feed bamboo to a panda
OR
give eucalyptus to a koala?

* * *

Visit the Eye of London
OR
the Taj Mahal?

* * *

Backpack across all of Europe
OR
go on a safari through Africa?

WOULD YOU RATHER...

Cross the Sahara Desert
OR
sail down the Amazon River?

* * *

Enjoy a bowl of Indian curry
OR
German eisbein?

* * *

Go to England to see Big Ben
OR
StoneHenge?

* * *

Visit an Aztec pyramid in Mexico
OR
an Egyptian pyramid?

* * *

Look for the Loch Ness monster in Scotland
OR
leprechauns in Ireland?

* * *

Go to a Mexican Day of the Dead festival
OR
Chinese New Year's festival?

* * *

Learn how to make pasta in Italy
OR
how to bake bread in France?

* * *

Get a set of Matryoshka dolls from Russia
OR
a cuckoo clock from Germany?

WOULD YOU RATHER...

Join Ali Babba and his thieves in Arabia
OR
Robin Hood and his Merry Men in Nottingham?
* * *
Visit Italy to see the Colosseum
OR
the Leaning Tower of Pizza?
* * *
Go to the Academy of Florence Art Museum in Italy
OR
the Louvre in Paris?
* * *
Attend a Carnival in Venice
OR
in Rio?
* * *
Visit the Cathedral of Notre Dame
OR
the Moscow Kremlin?
* * *
Pet a lemur from Madagascar
OR
play with an orangutan in Indonesia?
* * *
See the Parthenon in Greece
OR
the Pantheon in Rome?
* * *
Visit the Eiffel Tower in France
OR
the Tokyo Tower in Japan?

WOULD YOU RATHER...

Walk through an ancient feudal castle in Japan
OR
a fairy tale castle in Europe?

* * *

Eat a deep-fried tarantula
OR
soup made from boiling a bird's nest?

* * *

Go look for bigfoot in the American wilderness
OR
a yeti in the Himalayas?

* * *

Visit the Metropolitan Opera House in America
OR
the Sydney Opera House in Australia?

* * *

Go game watching in the Serengeti National Park
OR
see the geysers in Yellowstone National Park?

* * *

See the Great Wall of China
OR
the Wall of Berlin?

* * *

See the Golden Gate Bridge in San Francisco
OR
the Tower Bridge in London?

SUMMER

WOULD YOU RATHER...

Go on a tropical vacation in Hawaii
OR
the Caribbean Islands?
* * *
Build sandcastles at the beach
OR
watch sea creatures in an aquarium?
* * *
Get to taste every flavor of ice cream once
OR
eat as much as you want of a single flavor?
* * *
Go to the beach for a vacation
OR
go camping in the woods?
* * *
Visit a state fair
OR
spend a day at the pool?
* * *
Go to summer camp
OR
visit the Greek islands?
* * *
Get a bad sunburn at the beach
OR
get stung by a jellyfish?

WOULD YOU RATHER...

Go to the beach without your swimsuit
OR
go camping and bring nothing but your swimsuit?

* * *

Spend a month visiting a foreign family
OR
have someone foreign live with your family for a month?

* * *

Go to the beach but not be able to swim
OR
stay home and get to swim all you want?

* * *

Go camping for a week when it's raining every day
OR
stay home and it's sunny all day?

* * *

Get to go to the park every day for a week
OR
spend a week in a wildlife reserve?

* * *

Collect seashells on the beach
OR
look for interesting rocks and crystals in a cave?

* * *

Have your family own a summer vacation home
OR
go on a big overseas trip once?

* * *

Always have sand in your swimsuit
OR
always have a pebble in your hiking shoe?

WOULD YOU RATHER...

Go to Hawaii and stay in your hotel room
OR
stay at home and go wherever you want?

* * *

Wear an ugly hat all summer long
OR
stay indoors?

* * *

Fly a kite in the park
OR
read a book at home?

* * *

Go to a small amusement park every day for a month
OR
go to Disneyland for a week?

* * *

Have a pool in your backyard
OR
go to a trampoline park every day?

* * *

Take a walk along the beach
OR
take a walk in the woods?

* * *

Learn how to surf
OR
how to ride a horse?

* * *

Look for ancient ruins in a tropical jungle
OR
go exploring in a cave?

WOULD YOU RATHER...

Become a beach volleyball champion
OR
win a sandcastle competition?

* * *

Punch a shark on the nose
OR
win a wrestling contest with an alligator?

* * *

Cool down by only eating fresh summer fruits
OR
drinking soda with ice?

* * *

Spend the summer living in a treehouse
OR
on a houseboat?

* * *

Get a summer job on a ranch
OR
as a lifeguard?

* * *

Have a barbeque with your family
OR
make s'mores with your friends?

* * *

Go on vacation to a seaside resort
OR
a mountain lake resort?

WiNTER

WOULD YOU RATHER...

Get to sleep in an igloo
OR
a fur tent?
* * *
Be friends with a polar bear
OR
lead a flock of penguins?
* * *
Go to the North Pole
OR
the South Pole?
* * *
See the Northern Lights
OR
climb an iceberg?
* * *
Watch your favorite event in the Winter Olympics
OR
in your least favorite event in the Winter Olympics?
* * *
Have a snowball fight with an Eskimo
OR
build a snowman with a Viking?
* * *
Learn how to play ice hockey
OR
figure skate?

WOULD YOU RATHER...

Have a log fire in your hotel
OR
an electrical fire?
* * *
Go on a skiing trip and forget to bring your skis
OR
forget to bring a warm coat?
* * *
Spend your whole winter building one giant snowman
OR
a bunch of regular snowmen?
* * *
Go to an ice sculpture festival
OR
visit an outdoor Christmas market?
* * *
Swim in a volcanic hot pool in a snowy mountain
OR
swim in a frozen lake?
* * *
Tour a frozen forest on a dog sled
OR
go ice fishing?
* * *
Make the perfect snow anger
OR
win a giant snowball fight?
* * *
Spend your winter vacation on a beach
OR
a snowy mountain?

WOULD YOU RATHER...

Bring your gloves on a ski trip but not your scarf
OR
bring your scarf but not your gloves?

* * *

Visit Santa Claus in the North Pole
OR
see the biggest Christmas tree in the world?

* * *

Climb up a frozen waterfall
OR
pet a white reindeer?

* * *

Ride a snowmobile
OR
drive a horse-drawn sleigh?

* * *

Run a marathon in Antarctica
OR
explore an ice cave in Iceland?

* * *

Go whale watching in Hawaii
OR
visit an ice hotel in Sweden?

* * *

Go to a place where it's never winter
OR
where it's always winter?

* * *

Sled down a large mountain once
OR
down a small mountain several times?

WOULD YOU RATHER...

Spend the winter wearing a jacket that is a little too
big
OR
a little too small?

* * *

Have a winter vacation in a hotel that only serves hot
chocolate
OR
only serves apple pie?

* * *

Go on a holiday trip and have a cold the entire time
OR
stay at home and never get a cold?

* * *

Play a game of basketball outside in the snow
OR
try snowboarding indoors on fake snow?

* * *

Sit outside next to a bonfire
OR
stay inside in a heated room?

* * *

Be stuck inside a cabin where you're snowed in
OR
have no snow at all?

* * *

Eat all of the Christmas cookies you want but not get
any presents
OR
get lots of big Christmas presents but not get to eat
any cookies at all?

LANDSCAPES

WOULD YOU RATHER...

Visit Mount Fuji in Japan
OR
Mount Olympus in Greece?
* * *
See Niagara Falls
OR
go to the Grand Canyon?
* * *
Go on vacation to a lake
OR
climb a mountain?
* * *
Visit a wildlife preserve
OR
go to a bird park?
* * *
See the Harbor of Rio from Sugarloaf Mountain
OR
climb Mount Everest?
* * *
Swim in a volcanic hot spring in Iceland
OR
bathe in an oasis in the desert?
* * *
See the flat grass plains of Africa
OR
see the Alps?

WOULD YOU RATHER...

Spend winter in a desert
OR
summer in a frozen wasteland?

* * *

Have a vacation in a tropical jungle
OR
in a snowy forest?

* * *

Look at cherry blossoms in Japan
OR
jacaranda trees in South Africa?

* * *

Visit Stonehenge in England
OR
go to Easter Island in Chile?

* * *

Go hiking in the mountains
OR
go hiking in the woods?

* * *

Climb an ice glacier
OR
climb a canyon cliff?

* * *

Go to Europe and take a cruise on the Rhine river
OR
on the Danube river?

* * *

Go camping next to a lagoon near the ocean
OR
next to a lake deep inland?

WOULD YOU RATHER...

Visit Central Park in New York
OR
take a trip to Hyde Park in London?

* * *

Go cliff diving off of a waterfall
OR
take a boat ride on a subterranean river?

* * *

Sail down the Nile River
OR
sail down the Congo River?

* * *

Explore the Black Forest in Germany
OR
the Amazon Rainforest in Brazil and Peru?

* * *

Go to the Bayou in Florida Keys islands
OR
to the Okavango Delta in Botswana?

* * *

Go to Mount Etna to see an active volcano
OR
go to Mount Vesuvius?

* * *

Cross the Kalahari desert
OR
the Arabian desert?

* * *

Take a boat trip around the Horn Cape
OR
around the Cape of Good Hope?

WOULD YOU RATHER...

Visit a lavender field in France
OR
a tulip field in the Netherlands?
* * *
Get lost in the jungle
OR
be stranded in a desert?
* * *
Go island hopping in the Greek Isles
OR
in the British Isles?
* * *
Visit Iceland to see lava rivers
OR
look at ice glaciers?
* * *
Go camping in a tent
OR
go camping in a trailer?
* * *
Have a tropical island vacation in Hawaii
OR
in the Caribbean Islands?
* * *
Go cave spelunking in the Cave of the Crystals
OR
the Cradle of HumanKind?

OCEANS AND SEAS

WOULD YOU RATHER...

Cross the ocean in a yacht with a big group
OR
sail in a small boat all by yourself?
* * *
Go cage diving with sharks
OR
swim with dolphins?
* * *
Explore the Great Barrier Reef
OR
go deep-sea fishing?
* * *
Search for Treasure Island with Jim Hawkins
OR
explore the depths of the sea with Captain Nemo?
* * *
Become a lieutenant in the navy
OR
become the captain of a pirate ship?
* * *
Be lost at sea
OR
be stranded on a small island?
* * *
Find the lost city of Atlantis
OR
discover the secret of the Bermuda Triangle?

WOULD YOU RATHER...

Own a dolphin for a year
OR
spend a day with a mermaid?

* * *

Navigate the Pacific Ocean
OR
the Atlantic Ocean?

* * *

Discover a sunken ship while scuba diving
OR
explore an underwater cave?

* * *

Go swimming in the Red Sea
OR
in the Dead Sea?

* * *

Swim every day for a week in the ocean
OR
in a lake?

* * *

Swim with manta rays at night
OR
go diving for pearls during the day?

* * *

Talk to a whale
OR
ride a giant sea turtle?

* * *

Find buried treasure at the bottom of the ocean
OR
explore a giant blue hole?

WOULD YOU RATHER...

See a reenactment of a naval battle
OR
travel along a spice trading route?

* * *

Take a cheap cruise around the whole world
OR
an expensive cruise to one place and back?

* * *

Take a trip along the coast by road
OR
by ship?

* * *

Sail the seas on a pirate ship
OR
a Viking ship?

* * *

Join Bartolomeu Dias on his voyage to the Cape of
Good Hope
OR
Vasco da Gama on his voyage to India?

* * *

Cross to a new ocean through the Seuss canal
OR
through the Panama canal?

* * *

Go on a scuba diving trip in the Indian Ocean
OR
in the Arctic Ocean?

* * *

Go swimming in the icy North Sea
OR
the warm Mediterranean Sea?

WOULD YOU RATHER...

Go deep-sea diving
OR
snorkeling?

* * *

Explore the seas with a submarine
OR
an underwater jet ski?

* * *

Play with a seahorse
OR
pick up a sea star?

* * *

Explore a kelp forest
OR
an underwater river?

* * *

Cross the Strait of Gibraltar
OR
the English Channel?

* * *

Witness the naval Battle of the Red Cliffs
OR
the naval Battle of the Leyte Gulf?

* * *

Spend a week at sea with stale drinking water
OR
with stale food?

WEATHER

WOULD YOU RATHER...

Get caught in a sand storm in a desert
OR
in a snowstorm in the Antarctic?

* * *

Travel to somewhere warm
OR
somewhere cold?

* * *

Visit your favorite place and have horrible weather
OR
visit somewhere else and have perfect weather?

* * *

Travel somewhere that always has summer
OR
somewhere that always has winter?

* * *

Go on vacation to a tropical island
OR
to a desert?

* * *

Go to a place that has very hot summers and very cold
winters,
OR
a place that doesn't have any summer or winter at all?

* * *

Go somewhere where it always rains
OR
somewhere where it always snows?

WOULD YOU RATHER...

See a white rainbow in fog
OR
see a moonbow at night?

* * *

Watch the morning glory clouds in Australia
OR
see frost flowers in Japan?

* * *

See the Northern lights in Lapland
OR
the Southern Lights in New Zealand?

* * *

Run away from a waterspout at sea
OR
a fire whirl in a swamp?

* * *

Go somewhere where the sun shines at night
OR
somewhere where it's dark during the day?

* * *

Be able to control rain
OR
be able to control the temperature?

* * *

Visit a place that experiences a lot of hurricanes
OR
a place that experiences a lot of earthquakes?

* * *

Have your Hawaiian vacation interrupted by a tsunami
OR
a volcanic eruption?

WOULD YOU RATHER...

Eat ice cream on a sunny day
OR
eat pancakes on a rainy day?

* * *

Camp near a foggy lake
OR
on a cloudy mountain?

* * *

Save a town from a drought
OR
a flood?

* * *

Go somewhere where it rains in the winter
OR
the summer?

* * *

Have a warmer winter
OR
a colder summer?

* * *

See a lightning storm from far away
OR
from up close?

* * *

Have constant rain during a cruise
OR
no snow during a ski trip?

* * *

See snow in Israel
OR
a thunderstorm in Dubai?

WOULD YOU RATHER...

Have your dream vacation with perfect weather for one
week
OR
bad weather for a month?
* * *
Pay more for a trip during the best season
OR
pay less for a trip during the worst season?
* * *
Leave during the winter for a tropical vacation
OR
during the summer for a vacation in a snowy country?
* * *
Have a week of sunny weather in a place where it's
always cloudy
OR
a week of cloudy weather in a place where it's always
sunny?
* * *
Be refreshed by a cool evening breeze after a hot day
OR
warm your hands by the fire after building a snowman?
* * *
Be rescued from frostbite
OR
a sunstroke?
* * *
Go on vacation and know where you're going but not
what the weather will be like
OR
know what the weather will be like but not where you're
going?

WOULD YOU RATHER

GAME BOOK

For Kids 6-12 Years Old

CRAZY JOKES
AND CREATIVE SCENARIOS
FOR SPACE FANS

Lucky Sammy

SOLAR SYSTEM

WOULD YOU RATHER...

Fly through the rings of Saturn
OR
visit the asteroid belt?

* * *

Walk on the boiling surface of Venus
OR
sink through the gas of Saturn?

* * *

Discover a new planet
OR
live on the Moon?

* * *

Visit the Great Red Spot on Jupiter
OR
Olympus Mons on Mars?

* * *

Make a trip to the Sun
OR
visit the icy surface of Pluto?

* * *

See the Sun as it formed
OR
watch the Moon be created?

* * *

Watch the Earth orbit around the Sun
OR
the Sun orbit around Earth?

WOULD YOU RATHER...

Have a planet named after you
OR
rename Mercury after your pet?

* * *

Visit the site of a solar eclipse
OR
a lunar eclipse?

* * *

Get a tan on Mercury
OR
build a snowman on Neptune?

* * *

Live on a moon of Saturn
OR
on a colony on the Moon?

* * *

Turn Jupiter bright pink
OR
make the craters on the Moon purple?

* * *

Live on a super cold planet like Uranus,
OR
a super hot planet like Venus?

* * *

Live in the deepest crater in the solar system
OR
the tallest mountain in the solar system?

* * *

Gather space rocks from the asteroid belt
OR
the Kuiper belt?

WOULD YOU RATHER...

Visit a volcano on Venus
OR
on the moons of Jupiter?

* * *

Drink ice water from Mars
OR
the Moon?

* * *

Be in a hurricane on Earth
OR
on Jupiter?

* * *

Live on a deserted island on Earth
OR
be stranded on an asteroid?

* * *

Live on a planet with no atmosphere, like Mercury,
OR
one with too much atmosphere, like Venus?

* * *

Name asteroids after all of your friends
OR
give all of your friends a piece of a meteor?

* * *

Make friends with the Mars Curiosity Rover
OR
the Voyager probe?

* * *

Visit the Moon on vacation
OR
go live on Mercury?

WOULD YOU RATHER...

See a volcano on Mars
OR
an ice storm on Saturn?

* * *

Eat a piece of Moon rock
OR
a piece of Pluto?

* * *

Be able to see the solar system without a telescope
but not the Earth
OR
be able to see the whole Earth but not the solar
system?

* * *

Be a satellite orbiting the Earth
OR
a probe searching the whole galaxy?

* * *

Have dozens of moons orbiting around you that are
small
OR
one moon the same size as you?

* * *

Memorize a map of the moon
OR
a map of Mercury?

* * *

Travel north to see the Aurora Borealis
OR
stargaze for an hour to see a shooting star?

SPACE TRAVEL

WOULD YOU RATHER...

Travel to a galaxy far away
OR
explore the Milky Way?

* * *

Visit the Sun
OR
a star far away?

* * *

Visit a planet that is just like Earth
OR
one that breaks the laws of physics?

* * *

Travel faster than the speed of light
OR
time-travel to the past?

* * *

Discover water on a planet in the solar system
OR
life on a planet very far away?

* * *

Live on a planet that's all water
OR
a planet that's all rocks?

* * *

Get sucked into a black hole
OR
crash into a star?

WOULD YOU RATHER...

Be able to breathe without a spacesuit
OR
fly without a rocket ship?

* * *

Watch the sun exploding
OR
watch it forming?

* * *

Live on a planet with so much gravity you can't stand
up
OR
one with so little gravity that you float?

* * *

Visit the biggest star in the galaxy
OR
the smallest one?

* * *

Watch the solar system form
OR
the Sun explode?

* * *

Make the Sun change color to bright pink
OR
black?

* * *

Find a planet with only animals
OR
a planet with only plants?

* * *

Be able to teleport from planet to planet
OR
be able to breathe in any atmosphere?

WOULD YOU RATHER...

Use a spaceship with artificial gravity
OR
a ship with no gravity?

* * *

Visit a planet far away
OR
one close to Earth?

* * *

Take pictures of other planets with a telescope
OR
go there yourself?

* * *

Travel through space with your pet
OR
your siblings?

* * *

Drink water from a faraway planet
OR
eat the vegetables that grow on it?

* * *

Live on a spaceship
OR
live on another planet?

* * *

Live in a solar system with three stars
OR
a planet with three moons?

* * *

Discover a new planet
OR
a new star?

WOULD YOU RATHER...

Find a planet that's flat as paper
OR
one that's shaped like a donut?

* * *

Live on the first planet you land on
OR
move from planet to planet every day?

* * *

Visit a solar system with only gas giant planets
OR
a system with only rocky planets?

* * *

Find a new element on another planet
OR
discover life on one?

* * *

Live in a space station and go to work on the surface
OR
work at a space station and live on the surface?

* * *

Visit new galaxies in the past
OR
in the future?

* * *

Discover a planet ruled by cats
OR
one ruled by dogs?

ASTRONAUTICS

WOULD YOU RATHER...

Be the first person on the Moon
OR
the first person on Mars?

* * *

Be the captain of a spaceship
OR
the pilot?

* * *

Use a ship with faster than light travel and travel for a
few years
OR
be on a slower ship and sleep for the whole journey?

* * *

Command a battleship armed with missiles
OR
a science ship with all of the latest experiments?

* * *

Float through space in a spacesuit
OR
in a one-person spaceship?

* * *

Be in a spaceship with no windows
OR
one with constant turbulence?

* * *

Live in a space station that only orbits one planet
OR
on a ship that travels all the time?

WOULD YOU RATHER...

Take a ship to the Sun
OR
to Pluto?

* * *

Wear a spacesuit that is bright orange
OR
lime green?

* * *

Do a spacewalk on the International Space Station
OR
walk on the Moon?

* * *

Pilot a spaceship that looks like a minivan
OR
one that looks like a golf cart?

* * *

Be a member of the crew of the ISS
OR
the first mission to Mars?

* * *

Live on a colony on the Moon
OR
on Mars?

* * *

Visit a planet in person
OR
command a Rover from Earth?

* * *

Grow up in space
OR
raise your future kids in space?

WOULD YOU RATHER...

Have your parents become astronauts
OR
send your pet to the space station?
* * *
Go to school on a Moon colony
OR
on a faraway planet?
* * *
Eat freeze-dried astronaut food
OR
jello for every meal?
* * *
Be in the control center in Houston
OR
at the rocket launch in Florida?
* * *
Be the physicist making all of the calculations for the
spaceship
OR
the engineer putting everything together?
* * *
Fly through a field of asteroids
OR
the cloud of a nebula?
* * *
Be an astronaut yourself
OR
watch others as astronauts while you have another job?
* * *
Pilot a rocketship that can only fly left and right
OR
one that can only fly up and down?

WOULD YOU RATHER...

Command a ship where the only crew is other kids
OR
where you're the only kid?

* * *

Fly a spaceship with no brakes
OR
a spaceship with no engine?

* * *

Have your Captain be a robot
OR
an alien?

* * *

Do all of your space travel in our solar system
OR
in another galaxy?

* * *

Discover a planet with no life at all
OR
a planet run by spiders?

* * *

Have your spaceship travel slowly but you always know
where you're going
OR
travel through a wormhole with no idea what your
destination is?

* * *

Command a spaceship
OR
a colony on another planet?

PLANET EARTH

WOULD YOU RATHER...

Visit the top of Mount Everest
OR
the bottom of the Marianas Trench?
* * *
Live in the Amazon Rainforest
OR
the Sahara Desert?
* * *
Live in the North Pole with polar bears
OR
in the South Pole with penguins?
* * *
Discover a new species of plant
OR
a new species of animal?
* * *
Be a bug for a day
OR
a rodent for a day?
* * *
Learn to climb trees
OR
learn to scuba dive?
* * *
Eat an edible flower that tastes like candy
OR
an edible bug that tastes like chips?

WOULD YOU RATHER...

Be able to breathe underwater
OR
float in the air?

* * *

Be able to drink seawater from any ocean
OR
eat rocks from any continent?

* * *

Live on a farm with no one around
OR
in a big city with no nature close by?

* * *

Time travel 100 years to the future
OR
100 years to the past?

* * *

Time travel to meet the dinosaurs
OR
meet cavemen?

* * *

Learn to ride an elephant
OR
learn how to surf waves on the ocean?

* * *

Scuba dive in the Great Barrier Reef
OR
ski in the mountains of Colorado?

* * *

Hike up a steep mountain trail
OR
use a mountain bike to go up that trail?

WOULD YOU RATHER...

Walk a mile in nature every day
OR
drive 10 miles in open fields every day?

* * *

Have a national park named after you
OR
have a mountain named after you?

* * *

Drink the water from a glacier
OR
eat a plant from a rainforest?

* * *

Travel to the ancient ruins of civilizations in Egypt
OR
in Mexico?

* * *

Get turned into a flower in a botanical garden
OR
get turned into a fish in an aquarium?

* * *

Live in a house on your own private island
OR
live on the beach in a popular city?

* * *

Only be able to drink water from springs
OR
only be able to eat food grown in your backyard?

* * *

Travel across the world by flying
OR
by digging a tunnel underground?

WOULD YOU RATHER...

Discover the remains of a dinosaur
OR
the ruins of an ancient civilization?

* * *

Make friends with a dolphin
OR
a buffalo?

* * *

Live on a farm with cows
OR
in an orchard with apple trees?

* * *

Go to the bottom of the ocean
OR
to the bottom of the deepest valley on land?

* * *

Dig a hole to the center of the Earth
OR
take a ship to the top of the atmosphere?

* * *

Turn every pigeon in the world bright red
OR
make all butterflies five feet tall?

* * *

Invent flying cars
OR
invent a way to teleport?

ALiENS

WOULD YOU RATHER...

Have aliens come to Earth
OR
have our spaceships go to alien planets?

* * *

Discover that aliens are on every planet in the universe
OR
that life on other planets doesn't exist?

* * *

Speak an alien language
OR
learn an existing language you don't know?

* * *

Have aliens invade Earth and rule us
OR
invade an alien planet and rule them?

* * *

Meet an alien species that looks exactly like humans
OR
one that looks like a big blob?

* * *

Discover aliens in our solar system
OR
find them in a distant galaxy?

* * *

Get turned into an alien
OR
be best friends with one?

WOULD YOU RATHER...

Find out that your parents are secretly aliens
OR
that your family pet is a secret alien?
* * *
Go to a school where you're the only human student
OR
to a school where there's only one alien student?
* * *
Meet aliens who only speak in vowels
OR
aliens who only speak in consonants?
* * *
Discover aliens living on Mars
OR
deep underground on Earth?
* * *
Meet a species of alien that can shapeshift
OR
one that can fly?
* * *
Become an alien
OR
just meet them?
* * *
Have a universal translator so you can speak all alien
languages
OR
a teleporter so you can visit all alien planets?
* * *
Find an alien civilization that can only bark like dogs
OR
one that can only point at pictures to communicate?

WOULD YOU RATHER...

Discover aliens by them coming to Earth
OR
by us going to their planet?

* * *

Meet an alien species that can read each other's minds
OR
one that can move objects with their minds?

* * *

Have an alien become your adopted sibling
OR
your stepparent?

* * *

Discover aliens that have four arms
OR
ones that have six eyes?

* * *

Meet an alien species that only communicates with math
OR
one that only communicates with adjectives?

* * *

Find an alien planet full of kids
OR
one with only adults?

* * *

Introduce an alien to Earth food
OR
eat an alien's food that's nothing like food on Earth?

* * *

Discover that aliens built the Pyramids of Giza
OR
that aliens built the White House?

WOULD YOU RATHER...

Have your best friend be turned into an alien
OR
one of your parents turn into one?
* * *
Meet an alien who thinks you look gross
OR
meet an alien who you think looks gross?
* * *
Play hide-and-seek with an alien that can teleport
OR
play "the floor is lava" with an alien that can float?
* * *
Make a sports team made entirely of super tall aliens
play basketball
OR
football?
* * *
Discover an alien species that has no laws
OR
one that has so many laws they can't remember them
all?
* * *
Meet aliens who are ten feet tall
OR
ones that are ten feet wide?
* * *
Discover aliens living on Mercury who are immune to
heat
OR
discover aliens on Pluto who are immune to cold?

UNIVERSE

WOULD YOU RATHER...

Find a galaxy where all of the planets are forested
OR
one where all of the planets are oceans?
* * *
Discover a planet with only cats
OR
one with only dogs?
* * *
Find the place in the universe where gravity is the
strongest
OR
the place where it's the weakest?
* * *
Discover a galaxy that only has one planet in it
OR
a galaxy that has so many black holes it's impossible to
count?
* * *
Go through a black hole
OR
a wormhole?
* * *
See a star form
OR
see one die?
* * *
Discover that the universe is infinite
OR
that it has an ending point?

WOULD YOU RATHER...

Travel to the farthest galaxy from the Milky Way
OR
to the closest?

* * *

Go to a planet with too much gravity
OR
one with too little?

* * *

Have a nebula named after yourself
OR
after a galaxy?

* * *

Explore the edge of the Milky Way
OR
the center of it?

* * *

Live on the hottest planet in the galaxy
OR
the coldest one?

* * *

Find a galaxy that only has stars
OR
one that only has asteroids?

* * *

Discover a star so you can name it after yourself,
OR
discover a galaxy and name it after your favorite fictional
character?

* * *

Discover a galaxy that's shaped like a perfect circle
OR
one that is shaped like a spaghetti noodle?

WOULD YOU RATHER...

Have Earth be very close to another galaxy that you can see it during the day,

OR

so far away that you can only see the Milky Way?

* * *

Have the universe expand until everything is too far away,

OR

contract until all of the galaxies are right on top of each other?

* * *

Discover that the whole universe can fit into the palm of an alien's hand

OR

find out that it's all a dream?

* * *

Be in charge of the best telescope in the world

OR

be an astronaut on a one-way trip to other galaxies?

* * *

Watch two stars crash into each other

OR

two planets crash into each other?

* * *

Discover a volcano that takes up an entire planet

OR

a planet with one giant earthquake?

* * *

Live on a planet next to a black hole

OR

on a planet with no water?

WOULD YOU RATHER...

Try to fly a spaceship through a field of stars
OR
a field of black holes?

* * *

Be the first person to discover a star
OR
the first person to discover a galaxy?

* * *

Visit the smallest star in the universe
OR
the biggest one?

* * *

Get trapped in a nebula
OR
in an exploding star?

* * *

Find the perfect center of the universe
OR
the edge of it?

* * *

Turn a dozen stars into one gigantic star
OR
a dozen planets into one gigantic planet?

* * *

Watch the universe be created in the Big Bang
OR
watch it die?

* * *

Invent the best telescope ever
OR
the best spaceship ever?

NiGHT SKY

WOULD YOU RATHER...

Discover a constellation that looks like one of your
parents
OR
one that looks like your pet?
* * *
Only be able to find your way around using the stars
OR
using a compass?
* * *
Know the names of every constellation in the sky
OR
know the name of every star in the sky?
* * *
Meet the bear from the Big Dipper
OR
the bear from the Little Dipper?
* * *
Memorize your star sign
OR
your birthstone?
* * *
Discover a constellation all on your own
OR
be able to point out existing ones in the sky?

WOULD YOU RATHER...

Be able to see all of the stars without a telescope but you can't see during the day,
OR
be able to see during the day but unable to see any stars at night?

* * *

Meet the bull from Taurus
OR
the lion from Leo?

* * *

Have stars rotate around the Earth
OR
have the Earth rotate around all of the stars?

* * *

Find a constellation that looks like your favorite food
OR
one that looks like your favorite cartoon character?

* * *

Meet Perseus
OR
Hercules from their constellations?

* * *

See the Northern Lights no matter where you live
OR
be able to see the planets of the Solar System at all times?

* * *

Be able to see the Sun rotating
OR
be able to see Earth rotating?

WOULD YOU RATHER...

Switch day and night where you live
OR
switch the northern and southern hemispheres?

* * *

Be able to tell what day it is just by looking at the
stars
OR
be able to tell what time it is by looking at the
daytime sky?

* * *

Meet the flying horse from Pegasus
OR
the dolphin from Delphinus?

* * *

Name a constellation after your first name
OR
after your last name?

* * *

Have it pitch black outside at night so you can see the
Milky Way
OR
have lights on at night but you can only see the
brightest stars?

* * *

Live next to a powerful telescope on Earth
OR
live on a telescope in space?

* * *

Adopt the big dog from Canis Major
OR
the little dog from Canis Minor?

WOULD YOU RATHER...

Discover a constellation that looks like a car
OR
one that looks like an airplane?

* * *

Have every star in the universe be a part of a
constellation
OR
have no constellations at all?

* * *

Meet the twins from Gemini
OR
the crab from Cancer?

* * *

Find a constellation in the shape of a spider
OR
in the shape of a ghost?

* * *

Watch a meteor shower through a telescope
OR
look at Saturn's rings with that telescope?

* * *

See all of the constellations in the Northern
Hemisphere
OR
all of the ones in the Southern Hemisphere?

* * *

Look at stars in a traditional telescope
OR
look at the Sun through a solar telescope?

WOULD YOU RATHER...

Name a meteor after your favorite superhero
OR
name a constellation after your best friend?

* * *

Discover a constellation shaped like macaroni
OR
one shaped like a piece of cheese?

* * *

Meet the centaur from Centaurus
OR
the unicorn from Monoceros?

WOULD YOU RATHER

GAME BOOK

For Kids 6-12 Years Old

CRAZY JOKES
AND CREATIVE SCENARIOS
FOR YOUNG INVENTORS

Lucky Sammy

SCIENCE

WOULD YOU RATHER...

Discover a new planet in another solar system
OR
an underwater world on Earth?

* * *

Become a well-known scientist
OR
a famous inventor?

* * *

Find a cure for the common cold
OR
a cure for stinky farts?

* * *

Learn the science of dreams
OR
how nightmares work?

* * *

Smell stinky chemicals from a science experiment
OR
the stinky aroma of spoiled milk?

* * *

Invent a magical tonic to change the color of your skin
OR
the color of your hair?

* * *

Create a device that teaches animals to speak
OR
gives plants the ability to move?

WOULD YOU RATHER...

Conduct an experiment about loud sounds
OR
soft sounds?

* * *

Become a super-strong person
OR
a super-smart one?

* * *

Create slime that has a strange smell
OR
super sticky texture?

* * *

Discover a new kind of underwater plant
OR
a new kind of underwater creature?

* * *

Discover a new star
OR
a new moon?

* * *

Join a competition for young scientists
OR
young mathematicians?

* * *

Discover a meteor in your garden
OR
a fossil in your backyard?

* * *

Discover a new plant
OR
animal named after you?

WOULD YOU RATHER...

Be as slimy and warty as a frog
OR
as slow and steady as a snail?

* * *

Design unique scientific experiments
OR
create useful inventions?

* * *

Conduct an experiment about viruses
OR
fungi?

* * *

Discover a new element
OR
a new weather phenomenon?

* * *

Conduct experiments using man-made chemicals
OR
natural substances?

* * *

Invent something amazing and fun
OR
something incredible and scary?

* * *

Create an invention that allows you to jump all the way
to the sky
OR
run from one continent to another in a matter of
minutes?

* * *

Invent new things by yourself
OR
with your best friend?

WOULD YOU RATHER...

Make a potion that gives you the ability to camouflage
yourself
OR
turn totally invisible?
* * *
Discover a new scientific theory
OR
the answer to an existing scientific theory?
* * *
Invent a machine that can create new fruits
OR
vegetables using genetics?
* * *
Invent a device that can accurately predict earthquakes
OR
prevent them from happening?
* * *
Discover cures for diseases
OR
medications to make injuries heal faster?
* * *
Study animals by becoming a zoologist
OR
study plants by becoming a botanist?
* * *
Invent a device that reads other people's minds
OR
predicts your future?

TECHNOLOGY

WOULD YOU RATHER...

Play video games
OR
play outside with your friends all day?
* * *
Have a slow Internet connection all the time
OR
own a slow laptop?
* * *
Invent a mobile app
OR
a video game?
* * *
Fall on a prickly bush
OR
deactivate all of your social media accounts?
* * *
Live in a world without technology
OR
a world without people?
* * *
Read interesting eBooks
OR
watch captivating videos every single day?
* * *
Lose your smartphone
OR
break your laptop?

WOULD YOU RATHER...

Smell like a skunk forever
OR
lose your Internet connection forever?

* * *

Communicate with a ghost
OR
an alien through social media?

* * *

Download your brain into a computer
OR
a robot?

* * *

Invent the computer
OR
the smartphone?

* * *

Give up games
OR
social media?

* * *

Surf the Internet all day
OR
go to the movies with your friends?

* * *

Become a technological wizard
OR
a wizard with magic powers?

* * *

Have a thousand online friends
OR
a few real friends?

WOULD YOU RATHER...

Only have access to YouTube
OR
social media platforms like Instagram and Facebook?

* * *

Have an unlimited shopping spree
OR
access to unlimited screentime?

* * *

Explore the world virtually
OR
the real world without bringing any devices?

* * *

Post an embarrassing photo on social media
OR
eat a platter of boiled Brussels sprouts?

* * *

Become an app developer
OR
a super famous celebrity?

* * *

Play old-school games for free
OR
the newest games for a fee?

* * *

Get free food for the rest of your life
OR
free Internet?

* * *

Forget your homework
OR
your passwords?

WOULD YOU RATHER...

Catch a virus in your body
OR
on your computer?

* * *

Win ten million dollars
OR
a lifetime supply of gadgets and devices?

* * *

Use a computer to control an airplane
OR
a submarine?

* * *

Own a virtual house
OR
a virtual pet?

* * *

Take super easy written exams
OR
super challenging online exams?

* * *

Get lost in the woods with no signal
OR
no battery on your smartphone?

* * *

Become smarter than a computer
OR
faster than the speed of light?

ENGINEERING

WOULD YOU RATHER...

Only have math subjects
OR
drawing subjects in school?
* * *
Design space vehicles
OR
airplanes as an aeronautical engineer?
* * *
Create a design for a new car as an automotive engineer
OR
a design new machines as a mechanical engineer?
* * *
Create designs for ancient structures like pyramids
OR
modern structures like malls and office buildings?
* * *
Have all the money in the world
OR
become a well-known engineer?
* * *
Design the tallest building in the world
OR
the longest bridge in the world?
* * *
Become an engineer on Earth
OR
in outer space?

WOULD YOU RATHER...

Create fertilizers for planting crops
OR
chemicals for making medicines as a chemical engineer?
* * *
Go to the best school for engineers
OR
live in a huge mansion designed by a famous engineer?
* * *
Invent a machine that solves world hunger
OR
poverty?
* * *
Engineer something for your parents for free
OR
your best friend for a very high price?
* * *
Discover that you've become a whiz at mathematics
OR
a talented artist?
* * *
Work with computers as a computer engineer
OR
medical equipment as a biomedical engineer?
* * *
Invent a device that makes machines faster
OR
makes them work more efficiently?
* * *
Engineer a new type of car for kids to drive
OR
a new type of computer for kids to study with?

WOULD YOU RATHER...

Design communication devices for speaking underwater
OR
in outer space?

* * *

Build new things
OR
create designs for new things?

* * *

Learn how to help the environment
OR
how to make systems faster and smarter?

* * *

Be the most popular kid at school
OR
be the smartest one?

* * *

Learn how to become an engineer using books
OR
online videos?

* * *

Design a machine that makes all flavors of ice cream
OR
a computer that offers all types of games?

* * *

Spend the whole weekend sleeping and relaxing
OR
drawing and studying?

* * *

Engineer designs for people
OR
the environment?

WOULD YOU RATHER...

Get stranded with plenty of ideas but no materials
OR
plenty of materials but no ideas?

* * *

Spend your whole summer at math camp
OR
science camp?

* * *

Have natural intelligence
OR
natural talent?

* * *

Design plans for fast vehicles
OR
huge structures?

* * *

Discover problems to solve
OR
solutions to problems that other people discover?

* * *

Own a small company
OR
work with the biggest company in the country?

* * *

Create something that's noisy but useful
OR
something that's quiet but inefficient?

MATHEMATICS

WOULD YOU RATHER...

Do mathematical word problems
OR
number problems?

* * *

Only count backward
OR
walk backward for the rest of your life?

* * *

Forget how to recognize numbers
OR
the alphabet?

* * *

Learn how to calculate really fast
OR
decode messages really fast?

* * *

Eat half of an apple pie
OR
half of a meat pie?

* * *

Have outstanding logic skills
OR
superb common sense?

* * *

Be a master at solving puzzles
OR
an expert at making calculations?

WOULD YOU RATHER...

Be the best in class at fractions
OR
decimals?

* * *

Have the ability to remember all of your memories
OR
solve all types of math problems?

* * *

Carry one pound of nails
OR
one pound of feathers for an hour?

* * *

Be 20 minutes late
OR
40 minutes early for school every day?

* * *

Share a small bag of potato chips with one friend
OR
a big bag of potato chips with three friends?

* * *

Be 20% taller than you are now
OR
20% smarter?

* * *

Run a short maze within one minute
OR
a long maze with no time limit?

* * *

Get the credit for inventing pie
OR
pi?

WOULD YOU RATHER...

Have 10 bars of chocolate
OR
10 scoops of ice cream?

* * *

Master all the branches of mathematics
OR
speak all kinds of languages?

* * *

Decode a message using numbers
OR
symbols?

* * *

Count the number of tiles in your bathroom
OR
the number of shingles on your roof?

* * *

Have unlimited money
OR
unlimited time?

* * *

Learn how to guess lottery numbers
OR
combinations of safes?

* * *

Calculate five long problems by hand
OR
50 short problems using a calculator?

* * *

Forget how to add
OR
how to subtract?

WOULD YOU RATHER...

Learn how to tell time using only minutes
OR
seconds?

* * *

Tell time using Arabic numerals
OR
Roman numerals?

* * *

Perform calculations in your mind
OR
using a pencil and paper?

* * *

Lose 50% of your vision
OR
50% of your hearing?

* * *

Count coins
OR
paper bills in a vault?

* * *

Be the best in math but do badly in all other subjects,
OR
be the best in all other subjects but really bad at
math?

* * *

Learn all of the multiplication tables by heart
OR
have the ability to add big numbers in a flash?

PHYSICS

WOULD YOU RATHER...

Run faster than the speed of light
OR
speak louder than the loudest sound?
* * *
Have the power to turn back time
OR
stop it?
* * *
Become weightless
OR
be impervious to the effect of gravity?
* * *
Have more gravity
OR
less gravity when you're bouncing on a trampoline?
* * *
Feel too cold
OR
too hot all the time?
* * *
Study classical physics
OR
modern physics?
* * *
Visit a planet filled with gas
OR
a planet covered in ice?

WOULD YOU RATHER...

Win the Nobel Peace Prize
OR
the Breakthrough Prize in physics?
* * *
See sound waves
OR
light waves?
* * *
Go inside a black hole
OR
into a different dimension?
* * *
Watch the birth of a star
OR
the birth of a galaxy?
* * *
Visit the farthest planet
OR
the nearest star?
* * *
Get electricity for your home from water power
OR
wind power?
* * *
Invent the world's most powerful magnet
OR
a magnet that can attract non-metal objects?
* * *
Become a physicist who collects information
OR
develops theories?

WOULD YOU RATHER...

Travel to the past
OR
to the future?

* * *

Meet Galileo Galilei
OR
Sir Isaac Newton?

* * *

Have ultrasonic hearing
OR
X-ray vision?

* * *

Invent the wheel
OR
the light bulb?

* * *

Accelerate your vehicle using gas pedals
OR
by pedaling with your legs?

* * *

Discover the heaviest object that can float
OR
the lightest object that can sink?

* * *

Freeze like ice when it's sunny outside
OR
sweat buckets when it's cold outside?

* * *

See all of the colors of light in the spectrum
OR
see ultraviolet light with your eyes?

WOULD YOU RATHER...

Turn into liquid
OR
gas?

* * *

Invent a new kind of simple machine
OR
a new type of laser beam?

* * *

Have eyes that are powerful enough to see atoms
OR
ears that are sensitive enough to hear the softest
sounds?

* * *

Live without gravity
OR
without energy?

* * *

Become a master of physics
OR
a world-renowned chemist?

* * *

Fall into a bottomless pit
OR
a black hole?

* * *

Have your hair melt when it's hot
OR
have your face freeze when it's cold?

ROBOTICS

WOULD YOU RATHER...

Create a robot with genuine human emotions
OR
one with amazing superpowers?
* * *
Have a pet robot
OR
a pet dragon?
* * *
Invent a robot that can fly in the air
OR
a robot that can swim in the water?
* * *
Become an inventor of robots
OR
a tester of robots that others invented?
* * *
Live with a noisy robot
OR
one that makes loud sounds at unexpected moments?
* * *
Own a robot that gives off loud sounds
OR
speaks a strange language?
* * *
Encounter a dumb but friendly robot
OR
a smart but sinister one?

WOULD YOU RATHER...

Own a self-driving car
OR
a house that's completely automated?
* * *
Download your brain into a computer
OR
a robot that cannot move?
* * *
Meet an extraterrestrial life form that's mechanical
OR
one that looks like an animal or a human being?
* * *
Live on another planet with a colony of people
OR
a swarm of robots?
* * *
Be a world-famous robot
OR
an ordinary person?
* * *
Design a robot that controls the weather
OR
manipulates the seasons?
* * *
Invent a robot that can do cartwheels and other tricks
OR
one that tells the funniest jokes?
* * *
Invent a robot that will make you extremely rich
OR
genuinely happy?

WOULD YOU RATHER...

Discover a robotic life form that will help bring world
peace
OR
end world hunger?

* * *

Spend the rest of your life on an island with your best
friend
OR
a robot that cooks delicious meals?

* * *

Become a robot with limited mental capacity
OR
a virtual AI entity with no physical body?

* * *

Live with a robot that talks
OR
sings constantly?

* * *

Design a robot that provides you with unlimited free
Wi-Fi
OR
free food?

* * *

Have a robot friend that ages physically
OR
has a mind that deteriorates as time goes by?

* * *

Encounter a robot that will make you the most popular
kid in class
OR
one that will promise to be by your side forever?

WOULD YOU RATHER...

Invent a lifelike robot
OR
a new language that will unite the world?
* * *
Remain as a human who lives forever
OR
a robot that only lives for a hundred years?
* * *
Turn into a robot
OR
a car that thinks like a robot?
* * *
Dance "The Robot"
OR
speak with a robotic voice for the rest of your life?
* * *
Have a mechanical body with a human brain
OR
a mechanical brain with a human body?
* * *
Invent a robot that cleans your room every day
OR
cleans all the other rooms of your house except your
room?
* * *
Have a human-like robot friend
OR
an animal-like robot companion?
* * *
Discover a magic lamp
OR
an ancient robot when you explore a cave?

COMPUTERS

WOULD YOU RATHER...

Discover a computer that predicts the future
OR
gives you all of the answers to tests?

* * *

Unlimited battery life
OR
unlimited memory on your computer?

* * *

Use a super-fast computer
OR
a super lightweight one?

* * *

Have a computer that helps you understand all kinds of
animals
OR
languages from all over the world?

* * *

Invent a supercomputer for scientists
OR
explorers?

* * *

Create a computer that can control a spaceship
OR
an airplane?

* * *

Use a computer to catch bad guys
OR
discover a cure for a disease?

WOULD YOU RATHER...

Develop a computer game about a cat that uses its farts
to fly
OR
a mouse that uses its sneezes to move around on land?

* * *

Work on a super slow computer
OR
one that has short-term memory?

* * *

Never use a keyboard
OR
a touchscreen ever again?

* * *

Stop bathing
OR
give up using the Internet for one whole year?

* * *

Type at record speed
OR
be the fastest reader in the world?

* * *

Create the smartest computer in the world
OR
a new device that hasn't been invented yet?

* * *

Own a computer that's only meant for games
OR
social media?

* * *

Design a computer that can detect mental illnesses
OR
emotional distress?

WOULD YOU RATHER...

Become as smart as a computer while having to
recharge yourself every day
OR
being super strong with unlimited energy?
* * *
Learn how to make websites
OR
mobile apps?
* * *
Communicate with extraterrestrials through e-mails
OR
voice calls?
* * *
Stay up all night playing computer games
OR
learning new things on the Internet?
* * *
Use a computer to design an amusement park
OR
a mansion for the richest man on the planet?
* * *
Learn how to become a hacker
OR
a programmer?
* * *
Create a computer with built-in Wi-Fi
OR
with all kinds of computer games in the world?
* * *
Pay for an expensive computer
OR
an expensive robot?

WOULD YOU RATHER...

Receive a computer that will help you create a super-powered robot
OR
a new social media platform?

* * *

Be the best student at your computer subject
OR
be the best athlete in school?

* * *

Choose to give up computers
OR
sweet treats like ice cream and desserts?

* * *

Watch videos all day to learn what you need
OR
attend school in a traditional classroom?

* * *

Be the world's best video gamer
OR
the world's best program developer?

* * *

Live in a world without computers
OR
in a world without school?

* * *

Stay in your room alone with your computer forever
OR
get to explore the rest of your house but have to share your computer with your family?

WOULD YOU RATHER

GAME BOOK

For Kids 6-12 Years Old

CRAZY JOKES
AND CREATIVE SCENARIOS
FOR ACTIVE KIDS

Lucky Sammy

MUSiC

WOULD YOU RATHER...

Learn to sing
OR
learn to play an instrument?
* * *
Listen to country music
OR
to rock music?
* * *
Learn to play the piano
OR
the drums?
* * *
Play an electric guitar
OR
an acoustic guitar?
* * *
Meet your favorite singer or band and embarrass yourself,
OR
never meet them at all?
* * *
Be a backup singer for a band
OR
a backup dancer for a singer?
* * *
Start your own band with your friends,
OR
join a famous band with people you don't know?

WOULD YOU RATHER...

Listen to classical music
OR
to pop music?

* * *

Join a band and become the lead vocalist
OR
the lead guitarist?

* * *

Learn to play an electric guitar
OR
a bass guitar?

* * *

Listen to your favorite kind of music in a language you
don't understand,
OR
listen to your least favorite kind of music in your own
language?

* * *

Become a famous solo singer,
OR
be part of a famous band?

* * *

Go to live concerts a few times a year,
OR
listen to recorded music any time you want to?

* * *

Master the violin
OR
the cello?

* * *

Listen to only Taylor Swift music
OR
only to Justin Bieber music?

WOULD YOU RATHER...

Listen to music from One Direction
OR
the Jonas Brothers?
* * *
Go to a pop band live performance,
OR
see an orchestra performance?
* * *
Listen to choir music
OR
to acapella music?
* * *
Listen to your parents' favorite album of Queen
OR
The Beatles?
* * *
Get a tambourine
OR
a triangle as a present?
* * *
See a performance of authentic African music
OR
authentic Arabian music?
* * *
Know all the words to one of your favorite songs
OR
know a few words to a bunch of your favorite songs?
* * *
Learn to play a waltz
OR
to play a tango?

WOULD YOU RATHER...

Learn to play an instrument from someone who is very good but very strict,
OR
from someone who is only okay but very nice?

* * *

Never be allowed to sing your favorite song,
OR
only sing your favorite song and nothing else?

* * *

Listen to music on your own
OR
together with your friends?

* * *

Write songs for someone else to sing
OR
sing songs that someone else writes for you?

* * *

Listen to music while you're trying to relax
OR
while you're doing your homework?

* * *

Learn to play every musical instrument in the world
OR
invent your own musical instrument?

* * *

Only listen to music with just instruments
OR
music with singers?

SPORTS

WOULD YOU RATHER...

Play basketball
OR
baseball?

* * *

Be the best player ever in your least favorite sport
OR
the worst player in your favorite sport?

* * *

Join the football team
OR
the soccer team?

* * *

Learn to play tennis
OR
badminton?

* * *

Become a famous figure skater
OR
a famous hockey player?

* * *

Learn to snowboard
OR
learn to surf?

* * *

Try to play baseball with a tennis racket
OR
try to play tennis with a baseball bat?

WOULD YOU RATHER...

Become a famous sports star
OR
a famous athlete?

* * *

Have the new coach of your sports team be your mom
OR
your dad?

* * *

Be on a sports team with older kids
OR
with younger kids?

* * *

Become a beach volleyball champion
OR
a bowling champion?

* * *

Play a sport meant for the gym outside,
OR
a sport made for outside in the gym?

* * *

Watch your favorite sports game with your mom
OR
with your dad?

* * *

Play a sport in a team with just your best friend
against all your other friends,
OR
a team with all your friends but against your best
friend?

WOULD YOU RATHER...

Play baseball and hit a home run
OR
throw three strikes against all the batters on the other team?

* * *

Be good at dodgeball
OR
be good at chess?

* * *

Try to play soccer with a football
OR
try to play football with a soccer ball?

* * *

Be the captain of your sports team
OR
be the MVP of your sports team?

* * *

Be okay in your favorite sport but never practice,
OR
be great at your sport and practice every day?

* * *

Get soccer tips from Cristiano Ronaldo
OR
Lionel Messi?

* * *

Spend a day with your favorite local sports star
OR
an hour with your favorite international sports star?

* * *

Be the best pitcher on your baseball
OR
softball team or the best batter?

WOULD YOU RATHER...

Score points on your basketball team only by dunking
OR
only by scoring from behind the three-point line?

* * *

Watch your favorite game and have good seats for one game
OR
bad seats for 3 games?

* * *

Join a swimming club
OR
an equestrian club?

* * *

Play golf
OR
tennis?

* * *

Only play sports that are played outside
OR
sports played indoors?

* * *

Play a sport that is played in teams
OR
a sport that is played by one person on each side?

* * *

Become famous because you are a bad sports player,
OR
never become famous even though you're the best player on your team?

* * *

Be a good player on a bad team
OR
an okay player on a good team?

OUTDOOR ACTIVITIES

WOULD YOU RATHER...

Do incredible tricks with a skateboard
OR
with rollerblades?

* * *

Climb a tree
OR
swim in a lake?

* * *

Play tag
OR
hide and seek?

* * *

Ride a bicycle for a short while
OR
go for a long walk?

* * *

Feed bread crumbs to ducks
OR
nuts to squirrels?

* * *

Go to the park with your family
OR
with a group of friends?

* * *

Go camping in the back yard
OR
sleep in your treehouse?

WOULD YOU RATHER...

Play fetch with your dog
OR
catch with one of your parents or siblings?

* * *

Learn to ride a horse
OR
learn archery?

* * *

Go for a run in the woods
OR
along the beach?

* * *

Build a sandcastle in the summer
OR
a snowman in the winter?

* * *

Ride a horse
OR
go whale watching?

* * *

Go to the park for a picnic
OR
eat ice cream at the beach?

* * *

Grow a vegetable garden
OR
have a pond full of fish?

* * *

Spend a day fishing with your dad
OR
picking flowers with your mom?

WOULD YOU RATHER...

When hiking, would you rather have to slow down for your friends
OR
have to work hard to stay with the group?
* * *
Encounter a bear in the woods
OR
a shark in the ocean?
* * *
Go to a petting zoo
OR
a farm?
* * *
Bathe a horse
OR
shave a llama?
* * *
Go outside in the summer wearing a winter coat and mittens
OR
go outside in the winter wearing a t-shirt and shorts?
* * *
Spend the night stargazing
OR
watching a campfire?
* * *
Catch crabs at the beach
OR
frogs at the lake?
* * *
Have a three-legged race
OR
a water balloon fight?

WOULD YOU RATHER...

Paint using sticks and leaves
OR
draw a masterpiece in the sand?
* * *
Go bird watching
OR
try to catch a butterfly?
* * *
Find a strange plant
OR
a strange bug?
* * *
Wash your parent's car
OR
mow the lawn?
* * *
Win a snowball fight in the winter
OR
a water balloon fight in the summer?
* * *
Build an igloo
OR
a snowman?
* * *
Dig around in your yard and find buried treasure
OR
find dinosaur bones?

ARTS AND CRAFTS

WOULD YOU RATHER...

Fold a paper plane
OR
a paper boat?

* * *

Make a work of art with macaroni
OR
colored salt?

* * *

Become a famous painter
OR
a famous sculptor?

* * *

Build a bird feeder out of popsicle sticks
OR
make a Christmas star out of straw?

* * *

Make jewelry for your mom using clay beads
OR
paper beads?

* * *

Try to draw while holding your pencil with your mouth
OR
with your toes?

* * *

Make great art that no one gets to see
OR
make bad art that everyone sees?

WOULD YOU RATHER...

Use ribbons to make roses
OR
to make fish?

* * *

Color a picture using only your three favorite colors
OR
using anything except your three favorite colors?

* * *

Learn to knit
OR
learn to crochet?

* * *

Use old paper to create an interesting hat
OR
some pretty flowers?

* * *

Decorate a wall in your room with one big drawing
OR
lots of small drawings?

* * *

Draw pictures of people and animals
OR
draw pictures of places and things?

* * *

Use empty toilet paper rolls to make a snake
OR
a rocket?

* * *

Try to make a collage without using any glue
OR
cut out a picture without using scissors?

WOULD YOU RATHER...

Use yarn to make a wig
OR
to make a tail?

* * *

Paint pictures on flat rocks
OR
giant leaves?

* * *

Use old paper to make paper machE projects
OR
to make your own new recycled paper?

* * *

Go to your room
OR
somewhere outside to paint?

* * *

Use an egg tray to make a bird mask
OR
a little monster?

* * *

Master the art of origami
OR
the art of making felt animals?

* * *

Grow your own crystals inside an eggshell
OR
on a string?

* * *

Have a craft project ruined by someone spill juice on it
OR
by a cat knocking it off the table?

WOULD YOU RATHER...

Make a painting using only your handprints
OR
only your footprints?

* * *

Make a bar of soap
OR
make a fizzy bath bomb?

* * *

Make the world's most beautiful quilt
OR
the world's most beautiful tapestry?

* * *

Learn to make your own stuffed toys
OR
your own clay figures?

* * *

Use paper and glue to make a play sword
OR
a hand fan?

* * *

Make a scrapbook
OR
make a book full of collages?

* * *

Finish a dot-to-dot page
OR
a color by numbers page?

COLLECTiNG

WOULD YOU RATHER...

Collect strange rocks
OR
collect pretty seashells?

* * *

Display your collection of drawings and photos on your
wall
OR
in a photo album?

* * *

Have a shelf full of books
OR
full of sports trophies?

* * *

Collect rare stamps
OR
collect rare coins?

* * *

Have a big collection with nowhere to display it,
OR
a great display case but not enough items in your
collection?

* * *

Collect poisonous spiders
OR
poisonous scorpions?

* * *

Collect dinosaur bones
OR
dragon scales?

WOULD YOU RATHER...

Have a butterfly collection
OR
a beetle collection?

* * *

Collect rare playing cards
OR
signatures from famous people?

* * *

Share your collection with just your family
OR
with just your friends?

* * *

Have a large collection that no one gets to see
OR
have a small collection you get to show to anyone you
want?

* * *

Have a small collection all on your own
OR
have a large collection that belongs to your whole family?

* * *

Collect rare stuffed toys
OR
collect rare action figures?

* * *

Have a secret collection that's really embarrassing
OR
really gross?

* * *

Have a collection of really pretty plants
OR
really strange plants?

WOULD YOU RATHER...

Have a large collection of pens and pencils
OR
have a large collection of sketchpads and notebooks?

* * *

Collect as many different pennies from your home country
OR
collect a coin from as many different countries as possible?

* * *

Collect comic books
OR
video games?

* * *

Collect arts and crafts supplies
OR
toys?

* * *

Have a collection of model cars
OR
model airplanes?

* * *

Collect funny fridge magnets
OR
movie posters?

* * *

Have the rarest card in your card collection but nothing else,
OR
have all the cards in your collection except the rare ones?

WOULD YOU RATHER...

Collect toys and figurines from your favorite movie
OR
from your favorite cartoon?

* * *

Get a gift for your collection from your mom
OR
from your dad?

* * *

Make a collection of crafts your friends and family made
for you
OR
crafts you made yourself?

* * *

Have a collection with one of lots of different kinds of
things
OR
with a lot of different versions of one kind of thing?

* * *

Have a collection of your toenail clippings
OR
your fingernail clippings?

* * *

Collect footprints from different animals
OR
feathers from different birds?

* * *

Collect buttons of all shapes and sizes in one color
OR
collect buttons in one shape and size in lots of different
colors?

* * *

Have a collection of special gifts from your friends
OR
your family?

PERFORMING ARTS

WOULD YOU RATHER...

Become the world's greatest singer
OR
the world's greatest actor or actress?
* * *
Watch a musical on Broadway
OR
an Opera at the Metropolitan Opera House?
* * *
Grow up and join the circus
OR
the carnival?
* * *
Get a summer job in a traditional theatre
OR
a movie theatre?
* * *
Join the circus and learn to walk on the high wire
OR
perform on the flying trapeze?
* * *
Become a famous performer with a good reputation but
not a lot of talent
OR
with a bad reputation but a lot of talent?
* * *
Host a cooking competition
OR
a talent competition on television?

WOULD YOU RATHER...

Star in an action movie and do all your stunts yourself
OR
have a stuntman do all your stunts for you?

* * *

Become an actor or actress who only stars in movies
OR
only stars on series and cartoons?

* * *

Have your career as a famous performer start by being
discovered by a talent scout
OR
by winning a big talent competition?

* * *

Have your career as a famous performer end because of
a mistake you made
OR
a mistake someone else made?

* * *

Join the music club
OR
the drama club at school?

* * *

Become famous because of what you look and sound
like
OR
because of something you can do?

* * *

Work in the movies as a hair and makeup artist
OR
a costume designer?

WOULD YOU RATHER...

Get a job in your local theatre as a sound and lighting
technician
OR
as a stagehand?
* * *
Be the ringmaster of your own circus troupe
OR
the lead actor or actress in a play?
* * *
Join the school play and have a big role but get your
lines wrong when you perform
OR
get a small role and perform perfectly?
* * *
Become a famous ballet dancer
OR
a famous hip hop dancer?
* * *
Become a famous performer in a career you don't like
OR
stay an unknown performer in a career you love?
* * *
Become famous but not rich
OR
rich but not famous?
* * *
Become a dancer
OR
a gymnast?
* * *
Be a famous performer
OR
a famous sports star?

WOULD YOU RATHER...

Perform a song for your friends and forget the words
OR
sing the wrong melody?

* * *

Write and perform a play with your friends
OR
put on a talent show together?

* * *

Put on a special performance just for your friends
OR
just your family?

* * *

Enter a dancing competition and forget how to dance
OR
get all the dance steps wrong?

* * *

Join the school play and be blinded by the stage lights
OR
get stage fright?

* * *

Have your parents take you to watch a dog show
OR
a pony show?

* * *

Go to a movie festival
OR
a circus?

* * *

Become the world's funniest comedian
OR
the world's quietest mime?

GENERAL INTERESTS

WOULD YOU RATHER...

Own the perfect dog
OR
the perfect cat?

* * *

Have your favorite book turned into a movie
OR
have a book written about your favorite movie?

* * *

Have a longer weekend but spend more time at school
every day
OR
spend less time at school every day but have no
weekend?

* * *

Play with dolls with your little sister
OR
with cars with your little brother?

* * *

Travel all over the world
OR
go out into space?

* * *

Go on a trip to your favorite place in the world with
kids from school you don't really know
OR
have your friends visit you at home?

WOULD YOU RATHER...

Stay inside and make arts and crafts
OR
go outside and play?

* * *

Go to the petting zoo and spend the whole day with
one animal
OR
small parts of the day with all the animals?

* * *

Spend the afternoon playing video games
OR
board games with your friends?

* * *

Read a book
OR
watch a movie?

* * *

Have a parent teach you how to cook
OR
how to build things out of wood?

* * *

Eat the same three meals every day
OR
never eat the same thing twice?

* * *

Be the villain in your favorite movie
OR
the hero in your least favorite movie?

* * *

Be able to breathe fire
OR
turn things into stone by touching them?

WOULD YOU RATHER...

Take photos of all the places you go to
OR
draw pictures of them yourself?

* * *

Spend a whole day shopping with your mom
OR
with your dad?

* * *

Play outside with lots of regular friends
OR
with one best friend?

* * *

Be a monkey that can't climb trees
OR
a bird that can't fly?

* * *

Live in a big house but never get to go outside
OR
have a big yard but never get to go inside?

* * *

Have one hobby and be really good at it
OR
have lots of hobbies and only be okay at them?

* * *

Have an older sibling help you with your homework
OR
help a younger sibling with their homework?

* * *

Meet your favorite superstar actor,
OR
get to meet a character from your favorite book or
cartoon?

WOULD YOU RATHER...

Live closer to school but have to walk every day
OR
live a little further and ride your bike every day?
* * *
Live in a hut on the beach
OR
in a cabin on a mountain?
* * *
Have a really good console for video games but only have
games you don't like
OR
have all your favorite video games but not a nice console
to play them with?
* * *
Only ever watch movies
OR
only ever watch cartoons?
* * *
Time travel and go to the past
OR
the future?
* * *
Learn a completely new skill
OR
get even better at one of the skills you already have?
* * *
Get a hobby that lets you spend time with animals
OR
that lets you spend time with your friends?
* * *
Decorate your room any way you want
OR
get to keep any pet you want?

WOULD YOU RATHER

HALLOWEEN GAME BOOK

200+ Creative Questions,
Spooky Scenarios & Crazy Choices
For Kids 6-12 Years Old

Lucky Sammy

WOULD YOU RATHER...

Go to a haunted house
OR
have a picnic in a graveyard at midnight?
* * *
Get a single piece of candy
OR
get a basket filled with nothing but broccoli?
* * *
Make a costume yourself
OR
not have a costume at all?
* * *
Sleep in a vampire's coffin on Halloween,
OR
not sleep at all the entire night?
* * *
Be chased by a vampire who wants your candy and get away,
OR
give the vampire your candy and not run at all?
* * *
Be around a horde of real zombies dressed as one of them,
OR
walk in the streets with nothing but a full moon and a werewolf howling in the distance?
* * *
Be an angel for Halloween
OR
be a devil?

WOULD YOU RATHER...

Have a pumpkin as a head
OR
worms as fingers?

* * *

Go to a werewolf's house and get raw meat
OR
go to a Vampire's house and get fresh blood?

* * *

Turn into a ghost every Halloween
OR
stay human always?

* * *

Carve a pumpkin and eat its innards,
OR
dunk for apples and eat the stem and all?

* * *

Get cursed by a witch
OR
get chased by a pack of werewolves?

* * *

Dress up as a celebrity
OR
something spooky?

* * *

Resurrect Frankenstein's monster
OR
be ignored for a week?

* * *

Eat candy for breakfast for a week
OR
eat ice cream for dinner?

WOULD YOU RATHER...

Throw a party for the undead
OR
watch a scary movie alone?

* * *

Be a ghost hunter who fights the paranormal
OR
a ghost running from ghost hunters?

* * *

Wear the same cool costume as all of your friends
OR
wear a lame costume and be the only one wearing it?

* * *

Ride on a Unicorn's back but not be able to tell
anyone,
OR
eat an apple full of worms with the whole world
watching?

* * *

Carve one pumpkin the size of your house,
OR
10 smaller pumpkins the size of cars?

* * *

Have a bag full of chocolates that you are not allowed
to eat,
OR
a bag of apples that you are?

* * *

Visit a town where it's Halloween every day
OR
a town that doesn't know Halloween exists?

WOULD YOU RATHER...

Dress up as a witch and be human
OR
dress up as a human while being a witch?
* * *
Have a sleepover with Frankenstein's monster
OR
go to dinner at Dracula's house?
* * *
Fly on a broomstick
OR
craft potions in a cauldron?
* * *
Be surrounded by bats wherever you go
OR
walk in a fog for the entire night.
* * *
Live in a giant pumpkin that smells like a rotten apple
OR
live in a rotten apple that smells like a pumpkin?
* * *
Have to hang upside down from the ceiling to sleep at
night like a bat
OR
not sleep at all?
* * *
Read a scary book
OR
watch a scary movie?
* * *
Have to eat a platter of worms to get candy after
OR
eat nothing but cabbage for the entire night of
Halloween?

WOULD YOU RATHER...

Dig up a grave full of candy and have zombies chase
you,
OR
get only a basket of candy and stay safely at home?
* * *
Drink punch that tastes like blood
OR
drink blood that tastes like punch?
* * *
Wear a necklace of garlic and smell bad,
OR
smell good and be chased by vampires?
* * *
Have to eat an entire bag filled with candy corn,
OR
take your sibling trick or treating?
* * *
Have to dress up as a clown for the rest of your life
OR
never be able to leave your house ever again?
* * *
Be the one going trick
OR
treating or be the one giving out candy?
* * *
Have teeth the size of apples
OR
have fingers the size of teeth?
* * *
Have eyes the color of candy corns
OR
not have eyes at all?

WOULD YOU RATHER...

Pee your pants whenever you see something scary
OR
pee your pants whenever you see something funny?

* * *

Live in an abandoned asylum for the rest of your life
OR
never see another living being ever again?

* * *

Dress up as your dog
OR
dress your dog up as you?

* * *

Get candy corn
OR
chocolates?

* * *

Eat chocolate that croaks like a frog every time you
bite it
OR
eat chocolate that tastes like nothing at all?

* * *

Give up your mother's cooking forever to have candy
for the rest of your life,
OR
give up candy to have your mom cook for you forever?

* * *

Dress up as something you didn't want to be for
Halloween
OR
have your friends dress up as what you really wanted
to be?

WOULD YOU RATHER...

Laugh for the rest of your life
OR
turn to stone when the sun rises?

* * *

Prank someone who didn't give you candy and get in trouble
OR
clean up the mess someone else made as they pranked your house?

* * *

Have to share your candy with your friends
OR
not have friends at all?

* * *

Be an ingredient in a witch's brew,
OR
have garlic cloves for ears?

* * *

Get money that you can't spend when trick or treating
OR
get candy that you can't eat?

* * *

Watch a scary movie on TV
OR
at the movie theatre?

* * *

Watch the same funny movie every day for the rest of your life,
OR
watch a new scary movie every night?

WOULD YOU RATHER...

Do your friend's homework for a month for all their
candy
OR
give them all your candy so they'll do your homework?

* * *

Celebrate Halloween at school
OR
in a haunted house that you can't leave until dawn?

* * *

Go trick or treating with your teacher
OR
not go trick or treating at all?

* * *

Wear a hot mask and get a lot of candy
OR
wear something comfortable and not get any candy?

* * *

Crawl from door to door
OR
hop on one leg?

* * *

Fall and spill all of your candy on the floor
OR
get chased by a wicked witch on a broom?

* * *

Get caught in spider webs
OR
have a giant spider follow you around wherever you go?

WOULD YOU RATHER...

Have Halloween in winter
OR
summer?

* * *

Be followed by constant screaming
OR
constant laughing from a witch?

* * *

Sleep in a pile of raked leaves
OR
a haunted house?

* * *

Be the backside of a two-man unicorn costume,
OR
dress up as a toilet?

* * *

Get one candy bar every day for the rest of your life
OR
ten candy bars once a week?

* * *

Live 1000 years as a vampire, but you can't see your
friends ever again
OR
live for 50 years with all of your loved ones around you?

* * *

Be turned into a vampire
OR
a werewolf?

* * *

Wear a really itchy costume
OR
a costume that's too small?

WOULD YOU RATHER...

Be chased by someone dressed as a dentist
OR
a doctor?
* * *
Have your parents go trick or treating with you
OR
go alone?
* * *
Go trick or treating on a full moon
OR
new moon?
* * *
Howl at the moon
OR
turn into a bat?
* * *
Be what you dress up as for the entire night of Halloween
OR
be a human for that one night but be what your costume
is for the rest of your life?
* * *
Grow a third leg on Halloween
OR
grow ten extra fingers?
* * *
Eat a chocolate frog
OR
a gummy snake?
* * *
Have candy corn for teeth
OR
hot dogs for arms?

WOULD YOU RATHER...

Eat a real finger and nail
OR
a fake human being?

* * *

Be transported into your favorite movie every
Halloween,
OR
spend the night with your friends?

* * *

Decorate the house
OR
not decorate it at all?

* * *

Celebrate Halloween
OR
celebrate Easter?

* * *

Santa be a ghoul
OR
Halloween not be spooky?

* * *

Have a ghost take over your body every Halloween
OR
have that ghost haunt you for the rest of your life?

* * *

See the ghosts of passed loved ones
OR
see into the future?

* * *

Have a real fortune teller give you bad news
OR
a fake one giving you good news?

WOULD YOU RATHER...

Smell like bacon for the rest of your life
OR
not be allowed to trick or treat ever again?
* * *
Have a cape
OR
hood?
* * *
Fly with a witch
OR
run with a pack of werewolves?
* * *
Dance in the moonlight
OR
win a prize for best dressed?
* * *
Enter a costume contest but lose
OR
have an amazing costume but can't enter the contest?
* * *
Become a ghoul
OR
turn to stone?
* * *
Dress up as a Greek God
OR
a villain from a fairytale?
* * *
Celebrate Halloween at a waterpark
OR
a circus?

WOULD YOU RATHER...

Get buried alive
OR
never get buried at all?

* * *

Listen to spooky music for the rest of your life
OR
listen to smooth jazz on Halloween?

* * *

Be married to a monster
OR
a vampire?

* * *

Wear your Halloween costume for the rest of your life
OR
dunk for apples filled with worms?

* * *

Have a fake killer chase you
OR
a real killer in your friend-group?

* * *

Be mummified
OR
become immortal like a vampire?

* * *

Be cursed by a mummy
OR
be blessed by a fairy?

* * *

Become what you dress up as when you grow up
OR
be a real witch?

WOULD YOU RATHER...

Have pumpkins for ears
OR
go to a Halloween party all alone?

* * *

Know who everyone is beneath their masks
OR
knowing everyone's name when they are not in
costume?

* * *

Have a brother or sister take your candy
OR
have no candy at all?

* * *

Play video games
OR
eat candy?

* * *

Rake a whole garden of leaves
OR
put cobwebs up all over the house?

* * *

Eat a pie filled with fake guts
OR
watch a friend eat a pie filled with real ones.

* * *

Wear a full suit of armor
OR
ride a horse the entire night?

* * *

Be a supernatural being
OR
a superhero?

WOULD YOU RATHER...

Never be able to see yourself in a mirror
OR
never eat garlic ever again?

* * *

Be a fairytale character
OR
a dragon that spits fake fire?

* * *

Be recognized for your cool costumes
OR
your amazing personality?

* * *

Be in a Halloween themed band that only performs on
Halloween
OR
a normal band who's not allowed to perform at any
Halloween parties?

* * *

Decorate your room for Halloween
OR
only decorate the outside of your house?

* * *

Go to the grumpy old man down the street to trick or
treat
OR
just trick him without asking?

* * *

Carry around a fake broom
OR
wear fake wings?

WOULD YOU RATHER...

Wear makeup for Halloween
OR
a wig?
* * *
Drink punch
OR
have snacks and candy?
* * *
Get chips as treats
OR
candy?
* * *
Turn into a skeleton
OR
a zombie?
* * *
Wear a plunger on your head
OR
dress up as a toilet?
* * *
Meet new people while trick or treating
OR
trick or treat with your friends?
* * *
Create a brand new holiday and lose Halloween
OR
keep Halloween and lose all of the other holidays?
* * *
Dress up as a princess/prince
OR
a knight?

WOULD YOU RATHER...

Have webbed feet and hands like a frog
OR
eight eyes like a spider?

* * *

Be the one who haunts a house on Halloween
OR
tour the haunted house by yourself?

* * *

Carry a giant spider on your shoulder
OR
carry around a massive snake?

* * *

Feel a breath on your neck, but there is no one behind
you
OR
hear terrifying screaming, but not being able to find where
it's coming from?

* * *

Get bit by a zombie
OR
a vampire?

* * *

Trick
OR
treat?

* * *

Have dinner with a zombie
OR
a spooky movie character?

* * *

Wear a silly costume
OR
a scary one?

WOULD YOU RATHER...

See a black cat
OR
walk under a ladder?

* * *

Be friends with a werewolf
OR
a leprechaun?

* * *

Be terrifying all year round
OR
not be scary at all on Halloween?

* * *

Walk in the shadows
OR
hear footsteps behind you?

* * *

Have a pet owl
OR
a pet bat?

* * *

Constantly smell something rotten
OR
constantly walk on something rotten?

* * *

Eat an eyeball
OR
eat a tongue?

* * *

Explore a monster's lair in a dark forest
OR
have a monster explore your house?

WOULD YOU RATHER...

Go to bed early
OR
stay up to watch a spooky movie?

* * *

Go to school in a Halloween costume
OR
go to school in your pajamas?

* * *

Be chased by severed hands
OR
severed feet?

* * *

Be able to fly
OR
have a vampire's super-speed?

* * *

Walk like a zombie every Halloween
OR
crave brains like a zombie?

* * *

Be a white witch
OR
a black witch?

* * *

Drink a witch's concoction
OR
eat toad legs?

* * *

Play on a swing that threatens to break at every second,
OR
go to a haunted amusement park?

WOULD YOU RATHER...

Tell a ghost story around a campfire
OR
listen to ghostly cries while you are trying to sleep?

* * *

Hiss every second word
OR
purr every second sentence?

* * *

Find a scary clown in your bathtub
OR
a snake in your toilet?

* * *

Wear fake teeth
OR
fake ears?

* * *

Get a jump scare
OR
jump out of a closet and scare your parents?

* * *

Bathe in a tub of blood
OR
a tub of snail slime?

* * *

Be chased by a scarecrow
OR
a hoard of rats?

* * *

Kiss a toad
OR
eat a raw pumpkin?

WOULD YOU RATHER...

Get gifts on Halloween
OR
trick or treat on Christmas?

* * *

Have skeleton legs
OR
your face wrapped up like a mummy?

* * *

Find a nail in a pumpkin pie
OR
use a nail as a toothpick?

* * *

Go on an adventure with pirates
OR
discover a zombie?

* * *

Have your pet grow an extra head
OR
turn into a dragon?

* * *

Find a severed head
OR
a severed foot?

* * *

Turn into a frog for a day
OR
a zombie for a week?

* * *

Find out your computer is alive
OR
find a hidden room in your house?

WOULD YOU RATHER...

Have a talking dog
OR
a mummy dog?

* * *

Be a cat
OR
a bat?

* * *

Put your hand in a box filled with something unknown,
could be good, could be bad,
OR
put your hand in a box full of spiders?

* * *

Be an adult for a day
OR
be a vampire for a day?

* * *

Eat candy
OR
pumpkin pie?

* * *

Dream about Jack-o-Lanterns
OR
dream about cats?

* * *

Have only animal friends
OR
ghoul friends?

* * *

Talk to the dead alone
OR
the living alone?

WOULD YOU RATHER...

Find a witch's broom
OR
a wizard's wand?

* * *

Be able to eat an entire bag of candy
OR
all the pumpkin pie you want?

* * *

Have snakes able to slither on webs
OR
spiders the size of horses?

* * *

All cats turn into lions
OR
all bat decorations come to life?

* * *

Watch a movie about vampires
OR
a movie about a crazy doctor?

* * *

Be Frankenstein's monster
OR
Dracula's pet bat?

* * *

Have long, sharp nails
OR
vicious teeth?

* * *

Be able to see at night
OR
vanish in a puff of smoke?

WOULD YOU RATHER...

Become a zombie when you die
OR
be immortal and grow old and grey?
* * *
Eat cobweb candy floss
OR
chocolate-coated frogs?
* * *
Have black eyes
OR
white eyes?
* * *
Spend a night in Dracula's castle
OR
Frankenstein's lab?
* * *
Be a boy/girl for Halloween
OR
say "fart" before and after every sentence?
* * *
Be hunted by a demon
OR
followed by an annoying, whining ghost?
* * *
Eat an ice cream covered eyeball
OR
sugar a sugar-coated tongue?
* * *
Have a babysitter who's a vampire
OR
babysit a vampire?

WOULD YOU RATHER...

Forget Halloween
OR
forget your birthday?

* * *

Find toad eggs in your cereal
OR
have warts all over your face?

* * *

Have horns
OR
hooves?

* * *

Have a tail
OR
carry your head around in your hands?

* * *

Have teeth as eyelids
OR
eyelids as teeth?

* * *

Hear the cries of a banshee
OR
discover a unicorn?

* * *

See the future
OR
change the past?

* * *

Wear a witch's hat
OR
carry around a devil's pitchfork?

WOULD YOU RATHER...

Go back in time every Halloween
OR
get hunted by angry villagers?

* * *

Only have one tooth in the middle of your mouth
OR
have one eye in the middle of your head?

* * *

Wear ten layers of clothes
OR
evaporate in the sun like a vampire?

* * *

Have green skin like a witch
OR
be able to jump like a frog?

* * *

Be as venomous as a snake
OR
poisonous as a spider?

* * *

Have a talking skull nightlight
OR
talking cat sleeping at the foot of your bed?

* * *

Find out your neighbors are all ghouls
OR
be the ghoulish neighbors yourselves?

* * *

Lose a toe because a witch was chasing you
OR
lose a tooth because you bit into a bone in your candy?

WOULD YOU RATHER...

Crave brains
OR
crave live worms?

* * *

Prank a witch
OR
a werewolf?

* * *

Only be able to see when your eyes are closed
OR
only hear when your mouth is open?

* * *

Play piano on a skeletons' ribs
OR
play the flute on a witch's nose?

* * *

See other worlds through mirrors
OR
open doors to other dimensions?

* * *

Get trapped in darkness
OR
get trapped in a fog?

* * *

Hear chains dragging on the floor
OR
creepy crying?

* * *

Have glowing eyes
OR
glowing nails?

Made in the USA
Las Vegas, NV
15 June 2022

50251764R00098